FIREFIGHTER
COLORING
BOOK

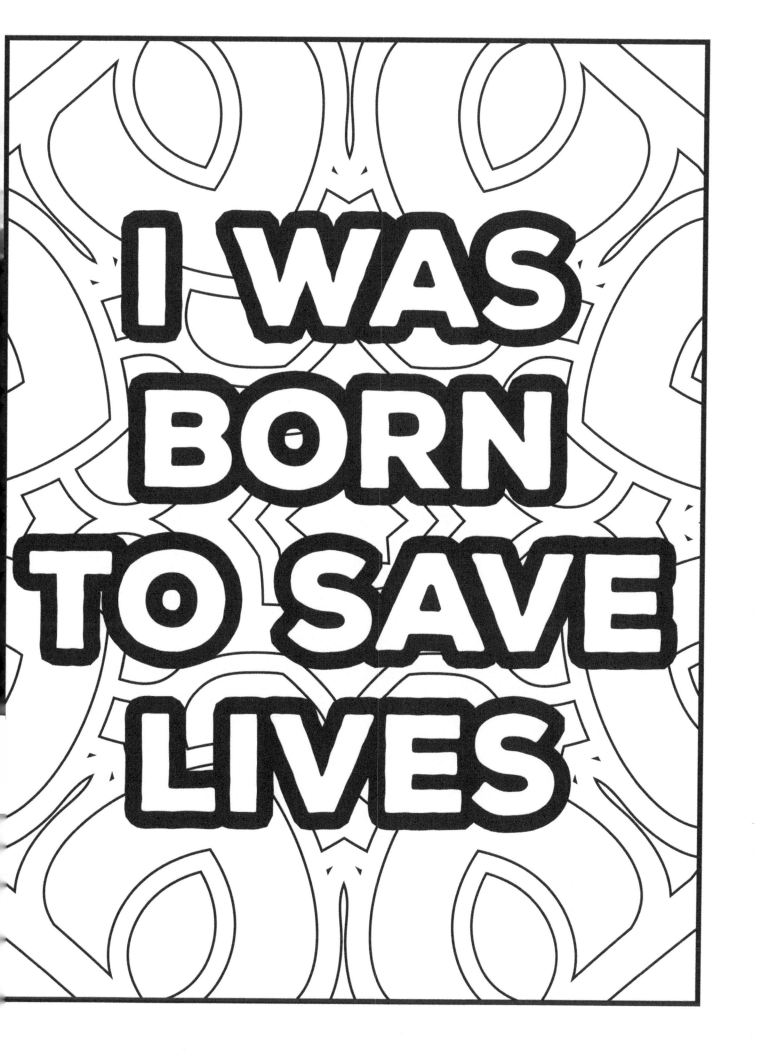

STRENGTH BEHIND THE BOOTS

911 IS MY WORK NUMBER

WHO NEEDS A SUPERHERO WHEN YOU'RE A FIREFIGHTER

THE BEST FIREFIGHTER EVER

Happiness is sliding up and down a fireman's pole

Made in the USA
Coppell, TX
27 August 2020